FAST FREDDIE

THE LEGEND IN A SHELL

★ BY MICHAEL HALE ★

To George who always wanted to go out into the desert,
and to Wally who always made sure we came back with a story.

To
Hailey &
Luca,

Keep
Exploring!

Michael
Hale

Published by Simian Books, LLC • 304 W. Gardenia Drive • Phoenix, AZ 85021
Copyright © 2019 © 2022 by Michael Hale
All rights reserved. No part of this book may be reproduced or copied in any form without written permission from the publisher. All other trademarks are the property of Simian Books, LLC.
Library of Congress Control Number 2019905501 • ISBN: 979-8-9864711-2-9
10 9 8 7 6 5 4 3 2
Design by Michael Hale
Printed in China.

In the high Sonoran Desert, where the tall saguaros grow,
there lived a little hatchling who was always on the go.

Federico was his name, but in the stories that they tell,
he's always called Fast Freddie, the legend in a shell.

A tortoise lives a quiet life. The same from day to day.

But Freddie wanted none of that.

So he stood up...

... **and ran away**.

With much to see and much to do, he wanted to explore.
To experience his desert home, like no one else before.

They say that he could run so fast,

he hardly touched the ground,

creating swirling dust devils each time he turned around.

Roadrunners were too slow for him.

Jackrabbits just like snails.

He left them all to eat his dust as he passed them on the trails.

Bighorn sheep have climbed to heights

that no one else would dare.

Montaña de la Tortuga.

But when they reached the summit,
they found Freddie waiting there.

He made many friends along the way.

Some easy to embrace.

While others, although very nice,

required extra space.

Always polite, he said, "No thanks"
and tried not to be rude

to dinner invitations, where
he might end up as food.

On overheated summer days, he'd hide out from the sun
and wait to join the nightlife, when the day was done.

Under clear and starry skies, he kept in perfect tune
along with the coyotes who were howling at the moon.

He had late night
chats with
friendly bats,

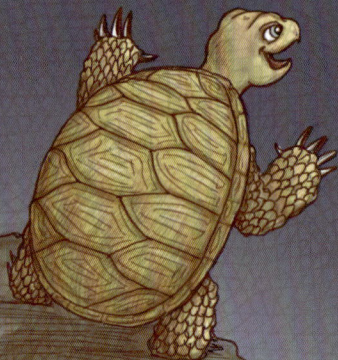

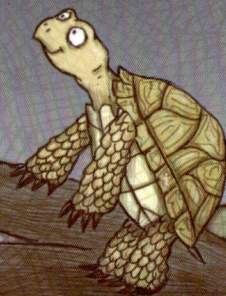

stare contests with owls.

and scared the gila monsters
with some pretty frightening scowls.

When the summer heat had lessened and the cacti fruit was ripe,

he'd eat his fill and dance a jig beneath an organ pipe.

He jogged with javelinas,

and would gamble with the quail.

And when it came to rattlesnakes... he really shook his tail.

During monsoon season, when water's flowing there,

DON'T TRY
THIS AT HOME!

he'd surf through the arroyos on a piece of prickly pear.

When he'd finally seen and done it all, with nowhere else to roam,
Freddie left the grand Sonora, his lovely desert home.

Before he went, to all his friends he bid a fond farewell.

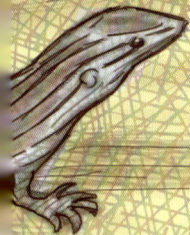

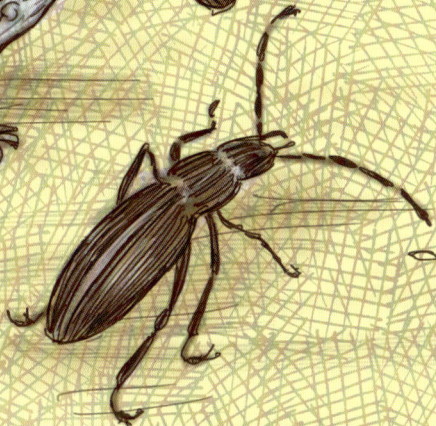

And to this day, they remember him.
The legend in a shell.

The last we'd seen, he'd headed west, toward the setting sun.
If anyone could catch it... it was Freddie on the run.

He took a brush and pails of paint... red, orange, yellow, gold

and every night the heavens glow in colors to behold.

The tall saguaro cacti's arms reach higher than the rest.

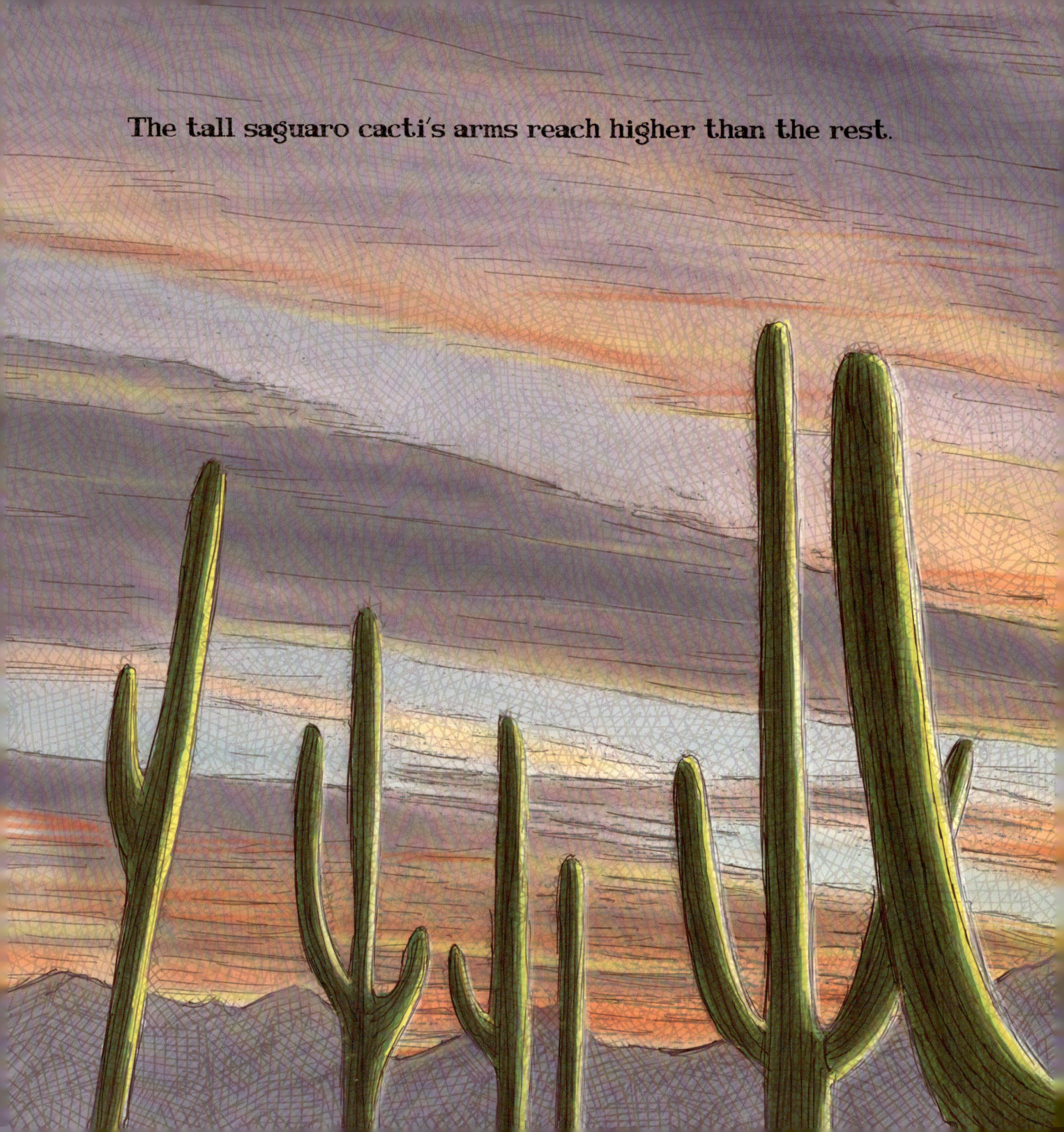

Some say they wave to Freddie
as the sun sets in the west.

Desert Tortoise (Gopherus morafkai)

The Sonoran Desert Tortoise is not a turtle. Unlike turtles that live in water, a tortoise spends its entire life on land. It has a large, dome shaped shell that can be up to 15 inches in length. It has a short tail, but it is not always visible. The back limbs are short, thick and rounded. They look like an elephant's legs.

The tortoise's forelimbs are flattened for digging. When threatened, it will pull its body and head into its shell and cover the opening with its thick, armored front legs.

Desert Tortoises are one of the most elusive inhabitants of the desert. They spend almost 95% of their time under ground to escape the heat of the summer and the cold of winter. They live in burrows, which they dig themselves. These burrows can be 3 to 6 feet deep. They will spend November through February hibernating underground.

They are most active in the daytime. As temperatures rise, they will wait until twilight to emerge and are occasionally active into the night.

They consume mostly plants. Feeding on grasses, cacti and other plant material. Most of their water intake comes from the plants and cacti that they eat, but during monsoon rains, they can be found drinking from pools of water.

Desert Tortoises mate from June through early August and lay a single clutch of up to 12 eggs. The eggs are usually buried inside the burrow. Once they hatch, the baby tortoises fend for themselves without any help from their parents.

Arizona Sunset

Arizona is famous for it's beautiful sunsets. Dry air and high clouds provide a perfect setting to showcase the many colors of the spectrum that make up white light. As the sun sets, those hues are filtered out by particles in the air and appear in vibrant color.

Arroyo

Also called a wash, a dry creek, stream bed or gulch. Arroyos are usually dry but will temporarily or seasonally fill up and flow with water after sufficient rain. Flash floods are common in arroyos following thunderstorms. The rushing water can be very dangerous. Stay out of them when it rains.

Bark Scorpion

These scorpions are found throughout the Sonoran Desert and are predators that consume insects. They are the only species of scorpion in Arizona whose sting is considered life-threatening to humans.

Coyotes

Coyotes will eat just about anything. In the Sonoran Desert coyotes vary their diet with the seasons. Coyotes howl as a way to communicate with other coyote families and as a way to keep track of their own family members.

Desert Bighorn Sheep

Desert Bighorn Sheep have adapted to the desert and can go for long periods of time without drinking water. Due to their unique hooves, Bighorn Sheep are able to climb the steep, rocky terrain of the desert mountains with speed and agility.

Diamondback Rattlesnake

When threatened, these venomous snakes coil and rattle to warn aggressors. They are one of the more aggressive rattlesnake species and stand their ground when confronted by a foe. If rattling does not work, the snake will strike in defense. If you encounter a rattlesnake, stop and back away slowly.

Gambel's Quail

Gambel's Quail are easily recognized by their top knots as they scurry along the desert floor. They are often followed closely by their young. The Gambel's quail is named in honor of William Gambel, a 19th-century naturalist and explorer of the Southwestern United States.

Gila Monster (HEE-la)

A heavy, typically slow-moving lizard, the Gila Monster is the only venomous lizard native to the United States. Although the Gila Monster is venomous, this sluggish reptile represents little threat to humans.

Jackrabbit

Jackrabbits can run at speeds up to 35 miles per hour. They are not actually rabbits but hares. They are same in size and form as rabbits, but generally have longer ears and live solitarily or in pairs. Unlike rabbits, their young are able to fend for themselves shortly after birth.

Javelina (HAH-vuh-LEE-nuh)

Also called Collared Peccaries, these medium-sized animals look similar to wild boars. However, they are not related to pigs. They live in large family groups that can range in size from 10 to up to 50 animals.

Lesser Long-nosed Bat

The endangered Lesser Long-nosed Bat survives on pollen and nectar from flowering plants. They have long tongues which they use to collect their food. Like bees, hummingbirds and other pollinators, they are vital to desert plant life as well.

Monsoon

A pattern of thunderstorms and rainfall over large areas of the southwestern United States. These storms typically occur between July and mid September.

Mountain Lion
Also known as a cougar or puma, the Mountain Lion is the top predator in the Sonoran Desert. These big cats prey on deer, javelina, big horn sheep, rabbits and many other small animals including the occasional tortoise.

Organ Pipe Cactus
This cactus species has several narrow stems that rise up from a single short trunk. It produces fruit about the size of a tennis ball. Under the fruit's spiny exterior is red flesh that has been described as tasting better than watermelon.

Prickly Pear Cactus
There are many varieties of prickly pear, a type of cactus with flat pads or paddles. Originally found only in the Americas, it now grows around the globe. In the southwest, it grows an edible fruit that is eaten by animals as well as humans.

Roadrunner
A fast-running ground bird related to cuckoos with a long tail and crest feathers. They can run over 20 miles per hour. Many Native American cultural traditions consider roadrunners to be medicine birds and protectors against evil spirits.

Saguaro Cactus (Sa-WAH-ro)
This cactus species is native to the Sonoran Desert and can grow to be over 40 feet tall. Saguaros have a long lifespan, often exceeding 150 years. Many desert animals rely on their fruit for food and make their homes in the cactus.

The Sonoran Desert
A North American desert which covers large parts of the southwestern United States in Arizona, California and Northwestern Mexico. The Sonoran Desert spans over 100,000 square miles and is one of the most diverse desert ecosystems in the world.

Western Desert Tarantula
Also known as the Arizona blonde tarantula, it is typically found in saguaro-dominated plant communities. Females are larger than males. Tarantulas are shy creatures that live most of their lives in burrows. Males can live up to 10 years of age, females up to 30.

Western Screech Owl
Western Screech Owls are cavity nesters, so you might see one peeking out of a hole in a saguaro cactus. They are silent nocturnal predators, feeding on rats, mice, lizards, insects, smaller birds, scorpions, spiders, and ground squirrels.